# MY TRAVELJOURNAL

London Sophia March 28

DATE: March 21    PLACE: home — hotel

## HOW I FELT TODAY:

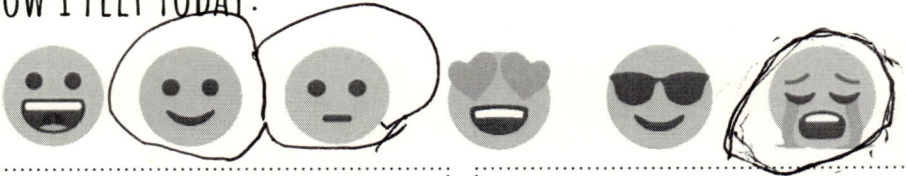

(emoji faces — 2nd, 3rd, and last circled)

## WHAT I'VE SEEN TODAY:

Edmonton, airport
airplane, red deer
Calgary, Montana
Wyoming, Colorado
texas, Gulf of Mex
Yucatan, cancun, and
Cansira,

## WHAT I ATE TODAY:

C.T.C. eggs, Kitkat
Pringues, (Rice)
Peas, S.B.

## HOW DID WE TRAVEL:

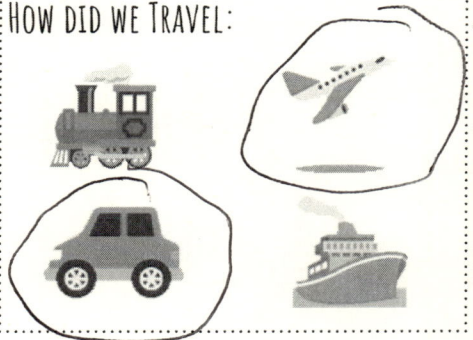

(train, car, airplane, and ship pictures — car and airplane circled)

## THE BEST THING THAT HAPPENED TOODAY:

at the hotel

## THE WEATHER TODAY WAS:

(sun and cloud pictures — both circled)

Date: March 22  Place: Hotel

## How I felt Today:

## What I've Seen today:
Beach, Pool, Me+Sand
water,

## What I Ate Today:

## How did we Travel:

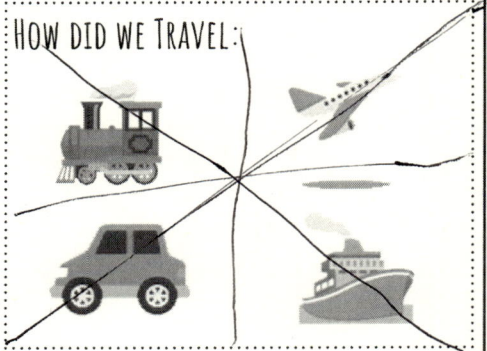

## The Best Thing that happened tooday:

## The Weather today was:

PLACE FOR DRAWINGS, PAINTINGS, WRITING, ENTRY TICKETS, PICTURES OR ALL THE OTHER STUFF YOU WANT TO CAPTURE

DATE: March 23  PLACE: Ocean

HOW I FELT TODAY:

WHAT I'VE SEEN TODAY:
pool, ocean, boats, sun, moon, people, sun, friends, family

WHAT I ATE TODAY:
Waffles

HOW DID WE TRAVEL:

THE BEST THING THAT HAPPENED TOODAY:
Dad and I everyone and waffles

THE WEATHER TODAY WAS:

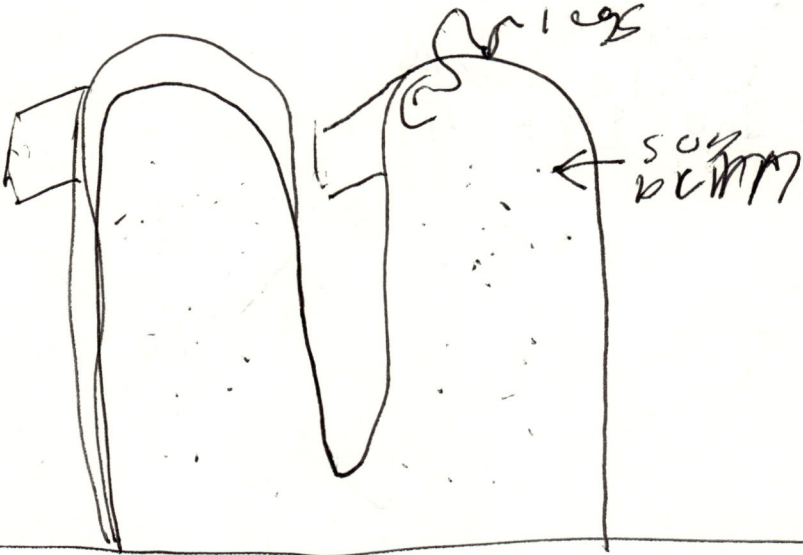

DATE: march 24   PLACE: Hotel (Pool)

## HOW I FELT TODAY:

(emoji selection — neutral face circled)

## WHAT I'VE SEEN TODAY:

(A) LOT
(of) stuff has
happened todos
and I kinda
just wanna wr not
not write about
my day, just write

## WHAT I ATE TODAY:

Waffles!!!!!!!

## HOW DID WE TRAVEL:

(all travel options crossed out)

## THE BEST THING THAT HAPPENED TOODAY:

Bingo! Waffles, sleeping in,

## THE WEATHER TODAY WAS:

(sun and cloud circled)

DATE: March 25   PLACE: Hotel - Pool

## HOW I FELT TODAY:

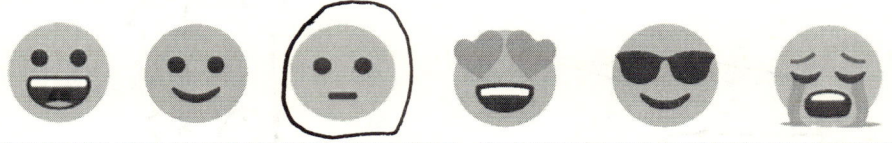

## WHAT I'VE SEEN TODAY:

when we went
to eat breakfast
we sat at a table
of 4 and I
put my water
down and then
went to get
when I came back
I could not find
our table so I went
to my mom and
we both couldn't
find it. Later we
found out they
put someone there!

## WHAT I ATE TODAY:

Waffles.

## HOW DID WE TRAVEL:

## THE BEST THING THAT HAPPENED TODAY:

## THE WEATHER TODAY WAS:

PLACE FOR DRAWINGS, PAINTINGS, WRITING, ENTRY TICKETS, PICTURES OR ALL THE OTHER STUFF YOU WANT TO CAPTURE

DATE: March 26   PLACE:

## HOW I FELT TODAY:

## WHAT I'VE SEEN TODAY:

_____
_____
_____
_____
_____
_____
_____
_____
_____
_____
_____
_____
_____
_____

## WHAT I ATE TODAY:

_____
_____
_____
_____
_____

### HOW DID WE TRAVEL:

## THE BEST THING THAT HAPPENED TOODAY:

_____
_____

## THE WEATHER TODAY WAS:

DATE: March 27  PLACE:

## HOW I FELT TODAY:

## WHAT I'VE SEEN TODAY:

_____
_____
_____
_____
_____
_____
_____
_____
_____
_____
_____
_____

## WHAT I ATE TODAY:

_____
_____
_____
_____
_____

## HOW DID WE TRAVEL:

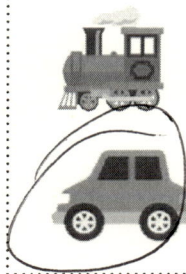

## THE BEST THING THAT HAPPENED TOODAY:

_____
_____

## THE WEATHER TODAY WAS:

PLACE FOR DRAWINGS, PAINTINGS, WRITING, ENTRY TICKETS, PICTURES OR ALL THE OTHER STUFF YOU WANT TO CAPTURE

DATE: march 8  PLACE:

## HOW I FELT TODAY:

## WHAT I'VE SEEN TODAY:

_____
_____
_____
_____
_____
_____
_____
_____
_____
_____
_____
_____
_____

## WHAT I ATE TODAY:

_____
_____
_____
_____
_____

### HOW DID WE TRAVEL:

## THE BEST THING THAT HAPPENED TOODAY:

_____
_____

## THE WEATHER TODAY WAS:

Place for Drawings, paintings, writing, entry tickets, pictures or all the other stuff you want to capture

**Date:**                    **Place:**

## How I felt Today:

## What I've Seen today:

_____
_____
_____
_____
_____
_____
_____
_____
_____
_____
_____

## What I Ate Today:

_____
_____
_____
_____
_____

## How did we Travel:

## The Best Thing that happened tooday:

_____
_____

## The Weather today was:

DATE: _____  PLACE: _____

## HOW I FELT TODAY:

## WHAT I'VE SEEN TODAY:

_____
_____
_____
_____
_____
_____
_____
_____
_____
_____
_____
_____

## WHAT I ATE TODAY:

_____
_____
_____
_____
_____

## HOW DID WE TRAVEL:

## THE BEST THING THAT HAPPENED TOODAY:

_____
_____

## THE WEATHER TODAY WAS:

Date: ............................ Place: ............................

How I felt Today:

What I've Seen today:
_____
_____
_____
_____
_____
_____
_____
_____
_____
_____
_____
_____
_____

What I Ate Today:
_____
_____
_____
_____
_____

How did we Travel:

The Best Thing that happened tooday:
_____
_____

The Weather today was:

PLACE FOR DRAWINGS, PAINTINGS, WRITING, ENTRY TICKETS, PICTURES OR ALL THE OTHER STUFF YOU WANT TO CAPTURE

DATE: PLACE:

HOW I FELT TODAY:

WHAT I'VE SEEN TODAY:
_____
_____
_____
_____
_____
_____
_____
_____
_____
_____
_____
_____

WHAT I ATE TODAY:
_____
_____
_____
_____
_____

HOW DID WE TRAVEL:

THE BEST THING THAT HAPPENED TOODAY:
_____
_____

THE WEATHER TODAY WAS:

**Date:**        **Place:**

## How I felt Today:

## What I've Seen today:

_____
_____
_____
_____
_____
_____
_____
_____
_____
_____
_____
_____

## What I Ate Today:

_____
_____
_____
_____
_____

### How did we Travel:

## The Best Thing that happened tooday:

_____
_____

## The Weather today was:

# Date:        Place:

## How I felt Today:

## What I've Seen today:

_____
_____
_____
_____
_____
_____
_____
_____
_____
_____
_____
_____
_____

## What I Ate Today:

_____
_____
_____
_____
_____

### How did we Travel:

## The Best Thing that happened tooday:

_____
_____

## The Weather today was:

Date: | Place:

## How I felt Today:

😃 😊 😐 😆 😎 😫

## What I've Seen today:

_____
_____
_____
_____
_____
_____
_____
_____
_____
_____
_____
_____

## What I Ate Today:

_____
_____
_____
_____
_____

### How did we Travel:

## The Best Thing that happened tooday:

_____
_____

## The Weather today was:

PLACE FOR DRAWINGS, PAINTINGS, WRITING, ENTRY TICKETS, PICTURES OR ALL THE OTHER STUFF YOU WANT TO CAPTURE

**DATE:** | **PLACE:**

## HOW I FELT TODAY:

## WHAT I'VE SEEN TODAY:

_____
_____
_____
_____
_____
_____
_____
_____
_____
_____
_____
_____

## WHAT I ATE TODAY:

_____
_____
_____
_____
_____

### HOW DID WE TRAVEL:

## THE BEST THING THAT HAPPENED TOODAY:

_____
_____

## THE WEATHER TODAY WAS:

Date: | Place:

## How I felt Today:

## What I've Seen today:

_____
_____
_____
_____
_____
_____
_____
_____
_____
_____
_____
_____

## What I Ate Today:

_____
_____
_____
_____
_____

## How did we Travel:

## The Best Thing that happened tooday:

_____
_____

## The Weather today was:

PLACE FOR DRAWINGS, PAINTINGS, WRITING, ENTRY TICKETS, PICTURES OR ALL THE OTHER STUFF YOU WANT TO CAPTURE

DATE: _____ | PLACE: _____

HOW I FELT TODAY:

WHAT I'VE SEEN TODAY:
_____
_____
_____
_____
_____
_____
_____
_____
_____
_____
_____
_____

WHAT I ATE TODAY:
_____
_____
_____
_____
_____

HOW DID WE TRAVEL:

THE BEST THING THAT HAPPENED TOODAY:
_____
_____

THE WEATHER TODAY WAS:

DATE: _____ PLACE: _____

HOW I FELT TODAY:

WHAT I'VE SEEN TODAY:

_____
_____
_____
_____
_____
_____
_____
_____
_____
_____
_____

WHAT I ATE TODAY:

_____
_____
_____
_____
_____

HOW DID WE TRAVEL:

THE BEST THING THAT HAPPENED TOODAY:

_____
_____

THE WEATHER TODAY WAS:

DATE: |  PLACE:

## HOW I FELT TODAY:

## WHAT I'VE SEEN TODAY:

_____
_____
_____
_____
_____
_____
_____
_____
_____
_____
_____

## WHAT I ATE TODAY:

_____
_____
_____
_____

## HOW DID WE TRAVEL:

## THE BEST THING THAT HAPPENED TOODAY:

_____
_____

## THE WEATHER TODAY WAS:

Date: ............................ | Place: ............................

How I felt Today:

What I've Seen today:
_____
_____
_____
_____
_____
_____
_____
_____
_____
_____
_____
_____

What I Ate Today:
_____
_____
_____
_____
_____

How did we Travel:

The Best Thing that happened Tooday:
_____
_____

The Weather today was:

PLACE FOR DRAWINGS, PAINTINGS, WRITING, ENTRY TICKETS, PICTURES OR ALL THE OTHER STUFF YOU WANT TO CAPTURE

# Date:                        Place:

## How I felt Today:

## What I've Seen today:

_____
_____
_____
_____
_____
_____
_____
_____
_____
_____

## What I Ate Today:

_____
_____
_____
_____

### How did we Travel:

## The Best Thing that happened tooday:

_____
_____

## THe Weather today was:

Place for Drawings, paintings, writing, entry tickets, pictures or all the other stuff you want to capture

Date: _____  Place: _____

## How I felt Today:

😃 🙂 😐 😎 😎 😫

| What I've Seen today: | What I Ate Today: |
|---|---|
| _____ | _____ |
| _____ | _____ |
| _____ | _____ |
| _____ | _____ |
| _____ | _____ |
| _____ | **How did we Travel:** |
| _____ | |
| _____ | |
| _____ | |
| _____ | |
| _____ | |

The Best Thing that happened tooday:
_____
_____

## The Weather today was:

Date: _____ Place: _____

How I felt Today:

What I've Seen today:

_____
_____
_____
_____
_____
_____
_____
_____
_____
_____
_____
_____

What I Ate Today:

_____
_____
_____
_____
_____

How did we Travel:

The Best Thing that happened tooday:

_____
_____

The Weather today was:

Place for Drawings, paintings, writing, entry tickets, pictures or all the other stuff you want to capture

Date: | Place:

## How I felt Today:

## What I've Seen today:

_____
_____
_____
_____
_____
_____
_____
_____
_____
_____
_____
_____

## What I Ate Today:

_____
_____
_____
_____
_____

## How did we Travel:

## The Best Thing that happened tooday:

_____
_____

## The Weather today was:

DATE: _____  PLACE: _____

## HOW I FELT TODAY:

## WHAT I'VE SEEN TODAY:

_____
_____
_____
_____
_____
_____
_____
_____
_____
_____
_____

## WHAT I ATE TODAY:

_____
_____
_____
_____
_____

## HOW DID WE TRAVEL:

## THE BEST THING THAT HAPPENED TOODAY:

_____
_____

## THE WEATHER TODAY WAS:

PLACE FOR DRAWINGS, PAINTINGS, WRITING, ENTRY TICKETS, PICTURES OR ALL THE OTHER STUFF YOU WANT TO CAPTURE

Date:                          Place:

How I felt Today:

What I've Seen today:

_____
_____
_____
_____
_____
_____
_____
_____
_____
_____
_____
_____

What I Ate Today:

_____
_____
_____
_____

How did we Travel:

The Best Thing that happened tooday:

_____
_____

The Weather today was:

PLACE FOR DRAWINGS, PAINTINGS, WRITING, ENTRY TICKETS, PICTURES OR ALL THE OTHER STUFF YOU WANT TO CAPTURE

DATE: _____  PLACE: _____

HOW I FELT TODAY:

What I've Seen today:

_____
_____
_____
_____
_____
_____
_____
_____
_____
_____
_____

What I Ate Today:

_____
_____
_____
_____
_____

How did we Travel:

The Best Thing that happened tooday:

_____
_____

The Weather today was:

PLACE FOR DRAWINGS, PAINTINGS, WRITING, ENTRY TICKETS, PICTURES OR ALL THE OTHER STUFF YOU WANT TO CAPTURE

**Date:** | **Place:**

## How I felt Today:

## What I've Seen today:

_____
_____
_____
_____
_____
_____
_____
_____
_____
_____
_____

## What I Ate Today:

_____
_____
_____
_____
_____

## How did we Travel:

## The Best Thing that happened tooday:

_____
_____

## The Weather today was:

Date: _____ | Place: _____

How I felt Today:

😀 🙂 😐 😍 😎 😩

## What I've Seen today:

_____
_____
_____
_____
_____
_____
_____
_____
_____
_____
_____

## What I Ate Today:

_____
_____
_____
_____
_____

### How did we Travel:

🚂 ✈️ 🚗 🚢

## The Best Thing that happened tooday:

_____
_____

## The Weather today was:

☀️ ☁️ ⛈️ 🌧️ 🌨️

PLACE FOR DRAWINGS, PAINTINGS, WRITING, ENTRY TICKETS, PICTURES OR ALL THE OTHER STUFF YOU WANT TO CAPTURE

Date: _____  Place: _____

## How I felt Today:

😃 😊 😐 😍 😎 😩

## What I've Seen today:

_____
_____
_____
_____
_____
_____
_____
_____
_____
_____
_____

## What I Ate Today:

_____
_____
_____
_____
_____

### How did we Travel:

## The Best Thing that happened tooday:

_____
_____

## The Weather today was:

# Date: _____ Place: _____

## How I felt Today:

## What I've Seen today:
_____
_____
_____
_____
_____
_____
_____
_____
_____
_____
_____

## What I Ate Today:
_____
_____
_____
_____
_____

## How did we Travel:

## The Best Thing that happened tooday:
_____
_____

## The Weather today was:

Date:                 Place:

## How I felt Today:

## What I've Seen today:

_____
_____
_____
_____
_____
_____
_____
_____
_____
_____
_____
_____

## What I Ate Today:

_____
_____
_____
_____
_____

### How did we Travel:

## The Best Thing that happened tooday:

_____
_____

## The Weather today was:

PLACE FOR DRAWINGS, PAINTINGS, WRITING, ENTRY TICKETS, PICTURES OR ALL THE OTHER STUFF YOU WANT TO CAPTURE

Date:            Place:

## How I felt Today:

## What I've Seen today:

_____
_____
_____
_____
_____
_____
_____
_____
_____
_____
_____

## What I Ate Today:

_____
_____
_____
_____

## How did we Travel:

## The Best Thing that happened tooday:

_____
_____

## The Weather today was:

Date: Place:

## How I felt Today:

## What I've Seen today:

_____
_____
_____
_____
_____
_____
_____
_____
_____
_____
_____
_____

## What I Ate Today:

_____
_____
_____
_____
_____

## How did we Travel:

## The Best Thing that happened tooday:

_____
_____

## The Weather today was:

PLACE FOR DRAWINGS, PAINTINGS, WRITING, ENTRY TICKETS, PICTURES OR ALL THE OTHER STUFF YOU WANT TO CAPTURE

DATE: | PLACE:

## How I felt Today:

## What I've Seen today:

_____
_____
_____
_____
_____
_____
_____
_____
_____
_____

## What I Ate Today:

_____
_____
_____
_____

## How did we Travel:

## The Best Thing that happened tooday:

_____
_____

## The Weather today was:

PLACE FOR DRAWINGS, PAINTINGS, WRITING, ENTRY TICKETS, PICTURES OR ALL THE OTHER STUFF YOU WANT TO CAPTURE

DATE:         PLACE:

## HOW I FELT TODAY:

## WHAT I'VE SEEN TODAY:

_____
_____
_____
_____
_____
_____
_____
_____
_____
_____

## WHAT I ATE TODAY:

_____
_____
_____
_____
_____

## HOW DID WE TRAVEL:

## THE BEST THING THAT HAPPENED TOODAY:

_____
_____

## THE WEATHER TODAY WAS:

Place for Drawings, paintings, writing, entry tickets, pictures or all the other stuff you want to capture

Date: | Place:

## How I felt Today:

## What I've Seen today:

_____
_____
_____
_____
_____
_____
_____
_____
_____
_____
_____

## What I Ate Today:

_____
_____
_____
_____
_____

## How did we Travel:

## The Best Thing that happened tooday:

_____
_____

## THe Weather today was:

PLACE FOR DRAWINGS, PAINTINGS, WRITING, ENTRY TICKETS, PICTURES OR ALL THE OTHER STUFF YOU WANT TO CAPTURE

**Date:** ............................ **Place:** ............................

**How I felt Today:**

😀 🙂 😐 😍 😎 😞

**What I've Seen today:**

_____
_____
_____
_____
_____
_____
_____
_____
_____
_____
_____
_____

**What I Ate Today:**

_____
_____
_____
_____
_____

**How did we Travel:**

🚂 ✈️
🚗 🚢

**The Best Thing that happened tooday:**

_____
_____

**THe Weather today was:**

☀️ ☁️ ⛈️ 🌧️ 🌨️

Place for Drawings, paintings, writing, entry tickets, pictures or all the other stuff you want to capture

DATE: | PLACE:

## HOW I FELT TODAY:

## WHAT I'VE SEEN TODAY:

_____
_____
_____
_____
_____
_____
_____
_____
_____
_____
_____
_____

## WHAT I ATE TODAY:

_____
_____
_____
_____
_____

## HOW DID WE TRAVEL:

## THE BEST THING THAT HAPPENED TOODAY:

_____
_____

## THE WEATHER TODAY WAS:

**Date:** _____ **Place:** _____

## How I felt Today:

## What I've Seen today:

_____
_____
_____
_____
_____
_____
_____
_____
_____
_____

## What I Ate Today:

_____
_____
_____
_____

### How did we Travel:

## The Best Thing that happened tooday:

_____
_____

## The Weather today was:

Place for Drawings, paintings, writing, entry tickets, pictures or all the other stuff you want to capture

Date: Place:

How I felt Today:

What I've Seen today:

_____
_____
_____
_____
_____
_____
_____
_____
_____
_____

What I Ate Today:

_____
_____
_____
_____

How did we Travel:

The Best Thing that happened tooday:
_____
_____

The Weather today was:

PLACE FOR DRAWINGS, PAINTINGS, WRITING, ENTRY TICKETS, PICTURES OR ALL THE OTHER STUFF YOU WANT TO CAPTURE

DATE: _____  PLACE: _____

## HOW I FELT TODAY:

## WHAT I'VE SEEN TODAY:

_____
_____
_____
_____
_____
_____
_____
_____
_____
_____
_____

## WHAT I ATE TODAY:

_____
_____
_____
_____

## HOW DID WE TRAVEL:

## THE BEST THING THAT HAPPENED TOODAY:

_____
_____

## THE WEATHER TODAY WAS:

Date:               Place:

## How I felt Today:

## What I've Seen today:

_____
_____
_____
_____
_____
_____
_____
_____
_____
_____
_____
_____
_____

## What I Ate Today:

_____
_____
_____
_____
_____

### How did we Travel:

## The Best Thing that happened tooday:
_____
_____

## The Weather today was:

PLACE FOR DRAWINGS, paintings, writing, entry tickets, pictures or all the other stuff you want to capture

Date:        Place:

## How I felt Today:

## What I've Seen today:

_____
_____
_____
_____
_____
_____
_____
_____
_____
_____
_____

## What I Ate Today:

_____
_____
_____
_____
_____

## How did we Travel:

## The Best Thing that happened tooday:

_____
_____

## THe Weather today was:

Place for Drawings, paintings, writing, entry tickets, pictures or all the other stuff you want to capture

Date: | Place:

## How I felt Today:

## What I've Seen today:

_____
_____
_____
_____
_____
_____
_____
_____
_____
_____
_____
_____

## What I Ate Today:

_____
_____
_____
_____
_____

## How did we Travel:

## The Best Thing that happened tooday:

_____
_____

## The Weather today was:

PLACE FOR DRAWINGS, PAINTINGS, WRITING, ENTRY TICKETS, PICTURES OR ALL THE OTHER STUFF YOU WANT TO CAPTURE

Date: _____ | Place: _____

## How I felt Today:

😃 🙂 😐 🤩 😎 😣

| What I've Seen today: | What I Ate Today: |
|---|---|
| _____ | _____ |
| _____ | _____ |
| _____ | _____ |
| _____ | _____ |
| _____ | _____ |
| _____ | |
| _____ | **How did we Travel:** |
| _____ | |
| _____ | |
| _____ | |
| _____ | |

## The Best Thing that happened tooday:

_____
_____

## The Weather today was:

☀️  ☁️  ⛈️  🌧️  🌨️

PLACE FOR DRAWINGS, PAINTINGS, WRITING, ENTRY TICKETS, PICTURES OR ALL THE OTHER STUFF YOU WANT TO CAPTURE

Date: _____  Place: _____

## How I felt Today:

## What I've Seen today:

_____
_____
_____
_____
_____
_____
_____
_____
_____
_____
_____
_____

## What I Ate Today:

_____
_____
_____
_____
_____

## How did we Travel:

## The Best Thing that happened Tooday:

_____
_____

## The Weather today was:

PLACE FOR DRAWINGS, PAINTINGS, WRITING, ENTRY TICKETS, PICTURES OR ALL THE OTHER STUFF YOU WANT TO CAPTURE

DATE: _____ | PLACE: _____

## HOW I FELT TODAY:

## WHAT I'VE SEEN TODAY:

_____
_____
_____
_____
_____
_____
_____
_____
_____
_____
_____

## WHAT I ATE TODAY:

_____
_____
_____
_____
_____

## HOW DID WE TRAVEL:

## THE BEST THING THAT HAPPENED TOODAY:

_____
_____

## THE WEATHER TODAY WAS:

Place for Drawings, paintings, writing, entry tickets, pictures or all the other stuff you want to capture

DATE:                PLACE:

## HOW I FELT TODAY:

## WHAT I'VE SEEN TODAY:

_____
_____
_____
_____
_____
_____
_____
_____
_____
_____

## WHAT I ATE TODAY:

_____
_____
_____
_____
_____

### HOW DID WE TRAVEL:

## THE BEST THING THAT HAPPENED TOODAY:

_____
_____

## THE WEATHER TODAY WAS:

PLACE FOR DRAWINGS, paintings, writing, entry tickets, pictures or all the other stuff you want to capture

Date: _____  Place: _____

## How I felt Today:

| What I've Seen today: | What I Ate Today: |
|---|---|
| _____ | _____ |
| _____ | _____ |
| _____ | _____ |
| _____ | _____ |
| _____ | |
| _____ | **How did we Travel:** |
| _____ | |
| _____ | |
| _____ | |
| _____ | |

## The Best Thing that happened tooday:
_____
_____

## THe Weather today was:

Date: Place:

## How I felt Today:

## What I've Seen today:

_____
_____
_____
_____
_____
_____
_____
_____
_____
_____
_____
_____

## What I Ate Today:

_____
_____
_____
_____
_____

## How did we Travel:

## The Best Thing that happened tooday:

_____
_____

## The Weather today was:

PLACE FOR DRAWINGS, PAINTINGS, WRITING, ENTRY TICKETS, PICTURES OR ALL THE OTHER STUFF YOU WANT TO CAPTURE

DATE:             PLACE:

## HOW I FELT TODAY:

## WHAT I'VE SEEN TODAY:

_____
_____
_____
_____
_____
_____
_____
_____
_____
_____

## WHAT I ATE TODAY:

_____
_____
_____
_____

## HOW DID WE TRAVEL:

## THE BEST THING THAT HAPPENED TOODAY:
_____
_____

## THE WEATHER TODAY WAS:

DATE: _____  PLACE: _____

## HOW I FELT TODAY:

## WHAT I'VE SEEN TODAY:

_____
_____
_____
_____
_____
_____
_____
_____
_____
_____
_____
_____

## WHAT I ATE TODAY:

_____
_____
_____
_____
_____

## HOW DID WE TRAVEL:

## THE BEST THING THAT HAPPENED TOODAY:

_____
_____

## THE WEATHER TODAY WAS:

**DATE:** _____    **PLACE:** _____

## HOW I FELT TODAY:

## WHAT I'VE SEEN TODAY:

_____
_____
_____
_____
_____
_____
_____
_____
_____
_____
_____
_____

## WHAT I ATE TODAY:

_____
_____
_____
_____
_____

### HOW DID WE TRAVEL:

## THE BEST THING THAT HAPPENED TODAY:

_____
_____

## THE WEATHER TODAY WAS:

PLACE FOR DRAWINGS, PAINTINGS, WRITING, ENTRY TICKETS, PICTURES OR ALL THE OTHER STUFF YOU WANT TO CAPTURE

Date: | Place:

## How I felt Today:

## What I've Seen today:

_____
_____
_____
_____
_____
_____
_____
_____
_____
_____
_____
_____

## What I Ate Today:

_____
_____
_____
_____
_____

## How did we Travel:

## The Best Thing that happened tooday:

_____
_____

## The Weather today was:

PLACE FOR DRAWINGS, PAINTINGS, WRITING, ENTRY TICKETS, PICTURES OR ALL THE OTHER STUFF YOU WANT TO CAPTURE

DATE:             PLACE:

## HOW I FELT TODAY:

## WHAT I'VE SEEN TODAY:

_____
_____
_____
_____
_____
_____
_____
_____
_____
_____
_____

## WHAT I ATE TODAY:

_____
_____
_____
_____

## HOW DID WE TRAVEL:

## THE BEST THING THAT HAPPENED TOODAY:

_____
_____

## THE WEATHER TODAY WAS:

PLACE FOR DRAWINGS, PAINTINGS, WRITING, ENTRY TICKETS, PICTURES OR ALL THE OTHER STUFF YOU WANT TO CAPTURE

Date: ........................... Place: ...........................

How I felt Today:

What I've Seen today:

_____
_____
_____
_____
_____
_____
_____
_____
_____
_____
_____

What I Ate Today:

_____
_____
_____
_____
_____

How did we Travel:

The Best Thing that happened tooday:

_____
_____

The Weather today was:

PLACE FOR DRAWINGS, PAINTINGS, WRITING, ENTRY TICKETS, PICTURES OR ALL THE OTHER STUFF YOU WANT TO CAPTURE

Date: | Place:

## How I felt Today:

## What I've Seen today:

_____
_____
_____
_____
_____
_____
_____
_____
_____
_____
_____
_____

## What I Ate Today:

_____
_____
_____
_____

### How did we Travel:

## The Best Thing that happened tooday:

_____
_____

## THe Weather today was:

jonathan kuhla
tempelhofer ufer 15
109 63 berlin
mail: jonathankuhla@gmail.com

Manufactured by Amazon.ca
Acheson, AB